This book belongs to

Lily

Dorling DK Kindersley

LONDON, NEW YORK, SYDNEY, DELHI, PARIS,
MUNICH, and JOHANNESBURG

Written by Sue Barraclough
Project Editor Fiona Munro
Designer Tanya Tween
Senior Editor Marie Greenwood
Managing Art Editor Jacquie Gulliver
Senior Managing Editor Karen Dolan
Production Nicola Torode

DTP Designer Andrew O'Brien
Picture Researchers Marie Osborne,
Andrea Sadler
Stylist Janis Morrison
Photographer Steve Shott

Illustrator Tony Watson

Barbie photography by Willy Lew, Shirley Ushirogata, Susan Kurtz,
Susan Cracraft, Judy Tsuno, and the Mattel Photo Studio

First American Edition, 2000

00 01 02 03 04 05 10 9 8 7 6 5 4 3 2 1

Published in the United States by Dorling Kindersley Publishing, Inc.
95 Madison Avenue, New York, New York 10016

Color reproduction by Media Development, UK
Printed in L.E.G.O., Italy.

Library of Congress Cataloging-in-Publication Data
Barbie: jobs to do. – 1st American ed.
   p.cm
  Summary: Uses Barbie, along with photographs and illustrations, to present a variety of careers, from ballerina
to landscape architect.
  ISBN 0-7894-6666-X
  1. Vocational guidance--Juvenile literature. 2. Occupations --Juvenile literature. [1. Occupations.] I. Dorling Kindersley, Inc.
HF5381.2.B33 2000
331.7'02'082--dc21

00-023244

The publisher would like to thank the following for their kind permission to reproduce their photographs:
Position key: c=centre; b=bottom; l=left; r=right; t=top
Allsport: Adam Pretty 28r; Gary Prior 17cr; Nick Wilson 17tl; Todd Warshaw 29tl; **American Museum of Natural
History:** 33cl; **Clive Barda:** 9tr; **British Museum:** 23l; **Bruce Coleman Ltd:** Leonard Lee Rue 20bl; **Colorsport:**
40cr, 40bl; **Corbis UK Ltd:** 19tl; **Sally & Richard Greenhill:** 46cr; **Mattel Uk Ltd:** 6cl, 10bl, 12r, 18tr, 20l, 22tr, 24r,
26r, 28l, 30tl, 32r, 34tl, 36l, 38cr, 40tl, 42tr, 44r, 46l, 48l; **Adrian Meredith:** 31tl; **Musee de L'Emperi:** 38tl; **N.A.S.A.:**
10tl, 10b, 10r; **Stephen Oliver:** 45tc; **PA News Photo Library:** 12cl, 38cl, 43tr; National Geographic Society, Brooks
Walker 32bl; **Redferns:** Mick Hutson 35tr; **Rex Features:** 13tl; Markus Zeffler 25tr; Sipa Press, Gerry Gropp 24bl;
Steve Wood 44tl; **Science Photo Library:** 23tc; **Frank Spooner Pictures:** B. Edelhajt 18br; Xinhua-Chine Nouvel
32cl; **Tony Stone Images:** 27tr, 35tl; Chad Slattery 30r; Don and Patti Valenti 26bl; **Telegraph Colour Library:** 36cr;
Neale Wilson 37tr; P. Tweedie 39tl; S. Benbow 22br; **Topham Picturepoint:** 45tl, 46br;

Dorling Kindersley would like to thank the following for appearing in this book:
Kelsey Birchmore, Zaynah Brown Hajjaj, Shanice Crawley, Jessica Ebsworth, Indiana Frankham,
Abigail Healy-Proctor, Charlotte Hole, Nicola Mooi, Vienna Prasher, Charlie Wooding,

see our complete
catalog at
www.dk.com

Barbie™
Career
Girl

A Dorling Kindersley Book

Contents

Computer Software Designer

Almost everyone uses computers today, either at work, in school, or at home. I design programs (or software) which tell computers how to do things. I work on my computer creating new CD-ROMs. Computers are changing all the time, so there is always something new to learn.

My laptop is useful to take into meetings or if I need to work at home

Brainstorming
Before a new CD-ROM is made, people get together to come up with ideas.

Coloring in
All the graphics (or pictures) are drawn on paper first. Then they are transferred to the computer and colored in.

Creepy crawly
A program was written to make these spiders move around the screen when you click on them. Can you spot a spider on the screen on the right?

This software designer is checking a series of numbers and letters (commands) that make up the program.

Does it work?
When pictures, sounds, and words have been put together, each command is checked using two screens. One shows the program code, the other shows the command being carried out on the CD-ROM.

Keyboard

Monitor

7

Mouse

CD-ROM

Computer

Ballerina

I always dreamed of becoming a ballerina and dancing on a spectacular stage in a beautiful costume. I began ballet lessons when I was very young and I go to classes every day. My *pointe* shoes have stiffened tips so I can dance on my toes.

Ballerinas usually have their hair tied back while rehearsing and performing

My pink tutu has a pretty skirt made of tulle

My ballet shoes are tied with satin ribbons

Warming up

At the beginning of a lesson, dancers do simple warm-up exercises, often holding onto a rail called a *barre*. Their teacher helps them perfect each movement.

1 2 3 4 5

First steps

These five positions for your feet are important because almost every step begins or ends with one of them. Each position has its own arm movement. Why don't you try them?

Starring role

Darcey Bussell is a principal ballerina, which means she is the star of the ballet. In this picture she is dancing a graceful *pas de deux* (a dance for two).

Ballet shoes

Dancing on a stage in front of hundreds of people is this ballet dancer's dream.

Arm movements are smooth and graceful

Hair is tied neatly on top of the dancer's head

Toes must always be pointed

Astronaut A

Earth

I had to train for many years to become an astronaut. It is amazing to zoom up in a space shuttle and see the Earth from hundreds of miles away. So far, people have only landed on the Moon, but one day planets much farther away will be explored.

Moving around
In space there is no gravity (the force which keeps your feet on the ground). It feels a little like moving around under water.

My suit has many different layers. The outer layer protects me against extreme temperatures and space dust

This tube is a lifeline. It is attached to my spacecraft and means that I can't float off into space and get lost!

Floating around
Astronauts' sleeping bags are strapped to the wall so they can't float away. It is difficult to eat when there is no gravity to keep your food on the plate!

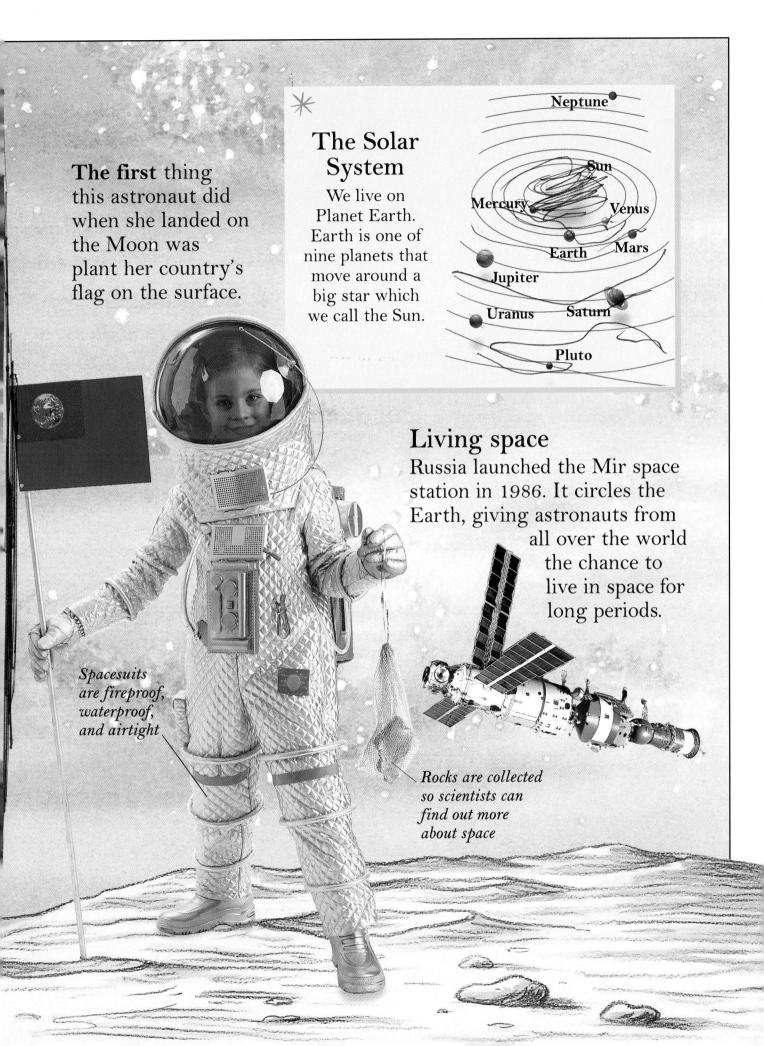

The first thing this astronaut did when she landed on the Moon was plant her country's flag on the surface.

The Solar System

We live on Planet Earth. Earth is one of nine planets that move around a big star which we call the Sun.

Neptune

Sun

Mercury

Venus

Earth

Mars

Jupiter

Uranus

Saturn

Pluto

Living space

Russia launched the Mir space station in 1986. It circles the Earth, giving astronauts from all over the world the chance to live in space for long periods.

Spacesuits are fireproof, waterproof, and airtight

Rocks are collected so scientists can find out more about space

Whistle

Police Officer

I am proud of my uniform because it shows people that I am there to help. I go out on the streets to patrol. You never know what's going to happen or when you may be needed, which makes every day different and exciting.

I can keep in touch with headquarters using my radio

I carry a notebook with me to write down things like car license-plate numbers

Comfortable shoes for patrolling the streets

Sniffing out crime

Police dogs are trained to follow instructions given by their trainer, and to track a scent to find people or things (such as drugs).

Solving crimes

When a crime is reported, the police make up a picture, or composite, of the suspect from a witness's description.

Make your own composites by cutting faces from magazines into strips showing hair, eyes, nose, and mouth then putting them in different combinations. Do any of them look like you?

12

Way up high

Being on horseback can be useful in large crowds. Because the police officer is so high up, it's easier to see what's going on. The horses are trained not to be frightened of traffic, crowds, or loud noises.

There has been an accident so this police officer has been called in to direct the traffic.

Police officers directing traffic wear white gloves so motorists can easily see their hands

Landscape Architect

Hand fork and flower pots

It is very rewarding to be able to turn an empty piece of land into a beautiful garden. First I measure everything carefully. Then I draw up detailed plans of how the finished area will look and which plants go where.

Pencils

Pond

Formal flowerbed

Picnic area

Flowerbed

A good plan
Gardeners use plans like this as they work. These must be drawn very carefully.

Play area

Pretty flowers

Look at these different plants and flowers. Which would you choose to grow in your garden?

Hydrangea

Chrysanthemums

Lupins

Rhododendron

Dahlia

Taking shape

Everyone working on a garden will follow detailed plans. When the work begins, the landscape architect visits regularly to sort out any problems.

The landscape architect will know which plants grow better in shade and which in sunlight

This landscape architect has nearly finished planting a garden she planned.

15

Each type of plant is placed according to the plans

Tennis Player

Tennis is a very exciting game. I love to play in tournaments, but it's hard work. I practice with my coach almost every day, to keep fit and improve my shots. One of the most difficult things is playing well in front of a big crowd of people.

Tennis racket

My tennis outfit is comfortable and easy to run in

This tennis player is practicing a volley. She stands with her legs slightly apart . . .

16

. . . keeps her knees bent . . .

My shoes have soles that grip the tennis court so I won't slip

. . . and her eyes on the ball . . .

. . . while tightly gripping her racket for a perfect shot!

Good shot!
All tennis players practice the same shot again and again. When playing in a match, their opponent will try to make them play their weakest shots.

Eye on the ball

When you begin to learn tennis it is important to practice keeping your eye on the ball. Throwing and catching games and bouncing a ball on your racket can help.

Double fun!

A doubles game is exciting to play and to watch. With four players on the court, the ball flies backward and forward over the net very fast.

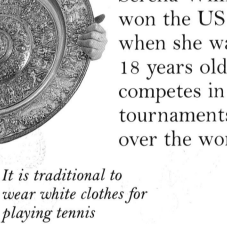

Star player

Serena Williams won the US Open when she was just 18 years old. She competes in tournaments all over the world.

It is traditional to wear white clothes for playing tennis

This tennis player has worked very hard to win the tournament.

Chef

Lobster salad

A hat keeps my hair covered

I have always loved cooking for my friends. When I graduated from high school I studied cooking at college and learned how to prepare and cook all kinds of different foods, and now I work in the kitchen of a big, stylish hotel. One day I would like to have a restaurant of my own.

The top part of my uniform is white. It is important to always look clean and neat

I wear comfortable shoes. I don't have much chance to sit down during the day!

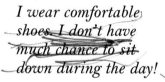

18

Chef's tool box

Chefs use lots of different tools when they are cooking. Do you have any of these things in your kitchen?

Scales

Blender

Garlic press

Oven mitt

Grater

Wooden spoon

Whisk

Saucepan

Chop, chop!

Before the restaurant opens, a lot of chopping and peeling has to be done so that dishes can be cooked quickly when they are ordered.

Cooked to order

In some restaurants food is cooked in front of the diners. A lot of Asian cooking uses very fresh ingredients that are prepared, cooked, and eaten very quickly.

This chef is slicing very quickly, but she must be careful because her knife is very sharp. Always ask for help if you are chopping or slicing at home.

A chef's tools are always stored where they can be found quickly and easily

A chef has to be very organized. She may need to do two jobs at the same time. This chef is cooking on the stove while chopping vegetables

Photographer

Film

I work as a photographer for a newspaper. The reporters plan a story, and if they want pictures, I go out to work with them. I carry lots of camera equipment so that I am ready for anything. I have to work and think fast, and know what will make a good picture.

I always carry spare film and lenses

Camera

Tripod

A tripod keeps my camera steady

How does it work?

Compact camera

1 Shutter release button – lets light in to take a photograph

2 Viewfinder – shows what will be in the photo

3 Flash unit – will light up a scene if there is not enough natural light

4 Lens – directs light onto the film

Risky pictures

Photographers who take pictures of wildlife need powerful lenses because it's dangerous to go too close.

Hold still!

In a studio, the photographer can make sure the lighting and the model's pose are just right. They often use several rolls of film just to get one perfect picture.

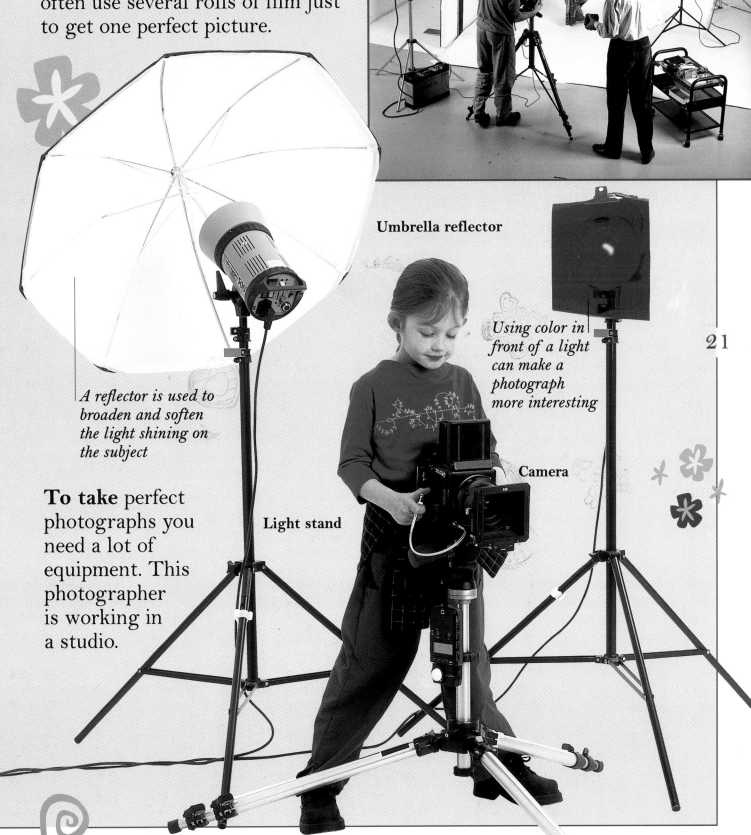

Umbrella reflector

A reflector is used to broaden and soften the light shining on the subject

Using color in front of a light can make a photograph more interesting

To take perfect photographs you need a lot of equipment. This photographer is working in a studio.

Light stand

Camera

21

Dentist

I enjoy caring for people's teeth and helping to keep them healthy. I show young children how to brush their teeth properly and give all my patients regular checkups. I have a special chair and use lots of different instruments to make sure that every tooth is clean and strong.

22

A white coat keeps my clothes clean

I show Kelly how to brush her teeth

White and bright

Take care of your teeth. Try to brush them after every meal.

Milk and fruit are good for your teeth.

Too much sugar is bad for your teeth.

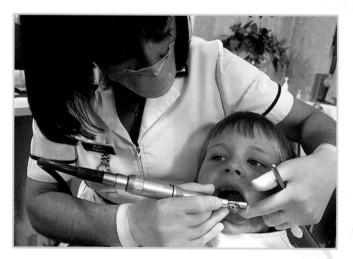

Open wide!

A dentist's chair can tilt up and down so that it is easy to see right into the patient's mouth. Most of the instruments are kept on a mobile tray so they are always within easy reach.

Smile please!

A dentist may take an X-ray (or photograph) of your teeth to see how they are growing and to check the roots.

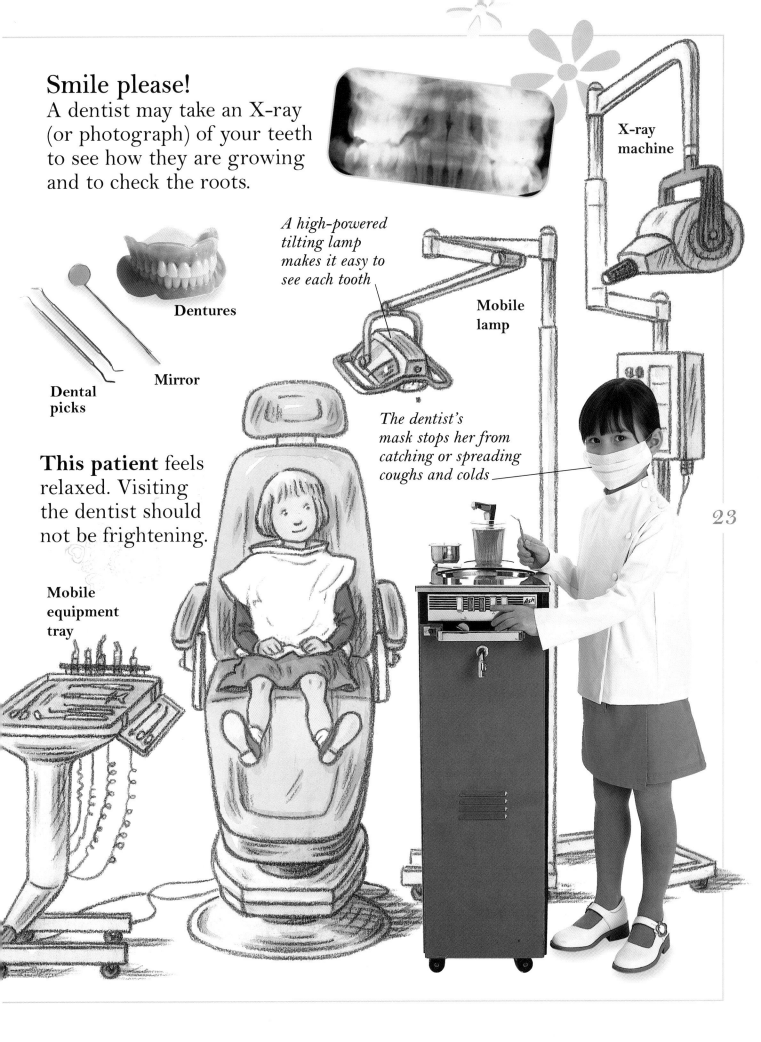

X-ray machine

Dentures

Mirror

Dental picks

A high-powered tilting lamp makes it easy to see each tooth

Mobile lamp

This patient feels relaxed. Visiting the dentist should not be frightening.

The dentist's mask stops her from catching or spreading coughs and colds

Mobile equipment tray

23

Politician

You can vote, too!

If you and your friends or family can't agree on something, draw up a voting paper, or ballot, for everyone. Each person puts a mark by their choice, and puts it in a box to be counted. The choice with the most marks wins!

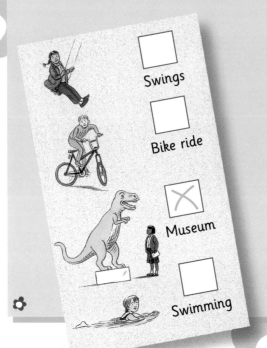

Swings

Bike ride

Museum

Swimming

I belong to a political party – a group of people with similar ideas about how a country should be run. We want people to vote for us so that we will become elected and have the power to change and improve things like schools, hospitals, and transportation.

My clothes are neat and businesslike

My briefcase is full of papers and reports for me to read

Vote for me!

When a political party is trying to get into power, they often tour the country persuading people to vote for them by explaining how their party plans to improve people's everyday lives.

Time to choose

An election is held to decide which party will run the country. People mark their ballots to select the party they want, then the ballot papers are collected and the votes counted. The party with the most votes wins the election.

This is the emblem, or symbol, which tells us the political party someone belongs to – each party has a different one

Newspaper and television reporters will report what the politician has to say

This politician is talking to a group of people. She is trying to persuade them to vote for her.

25

Teacher

Teaching is hard work, but I enjoy being with young children and helping them learn and understand new things. I teach a lot of different subjects to my class, including reading, writing, and counting. Every lesson is carefully planned so each day will be interesting for my students.

Calculator

Pen

Painting fun
All children enjoy art lessons! It's fun to paint your own pictures and learn about drawing. Do you take your pictures home to show your family? What was the last picture you painted?

These are the books I will be using today in class

It is important I set a good example to my students, so I always try to look tidy

Storytime
In many schools, teachers read a story to their younger students every day. This is a very popular part of the day and is a time when the whole class can be together.

Nature trail

Shells

Easel

Teachers sometimes give lessons away from the classroom so students can explore the places where animals and plants live and grow.

Starfish

This teacher is taking attendance. Every morning she calls out the names of the students in her class to check that they are all there.

Globe

Attendance book

Blackboard

Desk

The teacher sits at the front of her class. Students can go and talk to her at any time.

Basketball Player

Basketball is a very exciting sport. I train with my team almost every day so that we will play well together and win our games. Only five members of each team play at a time. If I'm not playing, I sit at the side of the court and cheer for the others.

The ball has a grainy surface so it's easier to catch

Basketball shoes have ankle supports

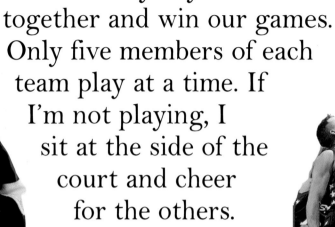

Fun for everyone

Many disabled people enjoy basketball. Wheelchairs can be specially adapted so players can move and turn quickly.

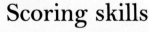

Scoring skills

Here are three of the skills you will need. The aim of the game is to throw the ball into the basket.

Bounce the ball as you run while trying to stop the other team from getting the ball. This is called dribbling

Throw the ball to other players on your team. This is called passing

Put the ball into the hoop to score. This is called shooting

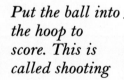

Score!

In a game, points are scored by putting the ball through the hoop.

Backboard

It takes skill and practice to get past your opponent and score

Hoop

This basketball player is jumping up high to shoot a basket for her team.

A player wears a jersey and shorts in the colors of her team

29

At important games, photographers stand at the side of the court and take pictures. These will be in the next day's newspapers

Airline Pilot

Flying a plane full of passengers and crew is a very important job. I am one of a team of people who work together to make sure all our passengers have a safe and comfortable journey. I fly all over the world and visit lots of interesting countries.

Takeoff!

At every airport there is an air traffic control tower. Controllers talk to the pilots and make sure that planes come and go safely. At a big airport there will be planes taking off and landing every few seconds.

My bag contains maps and charts needed for the journey

The airline I work for has a very stylish uniform

What's inside?

A passenger plane has to be well designed because there is a lot to fit inside it.

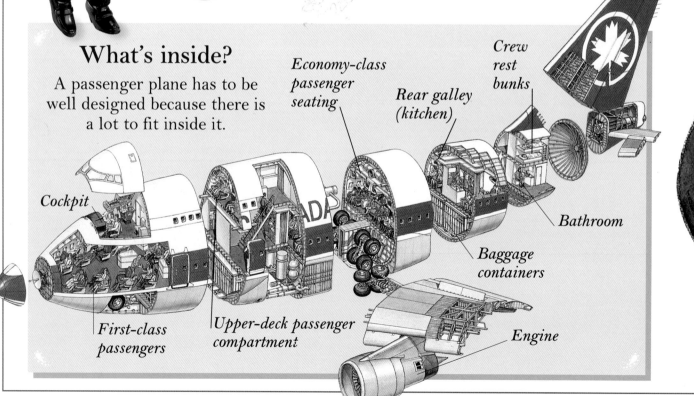

Economy-class passenger seating

Rear galley (kitchen)

Crew rest bunks

Bathroom

Baggage containers

Cockpit

First-class passengers

Upper-deck passenger compartment

Engine

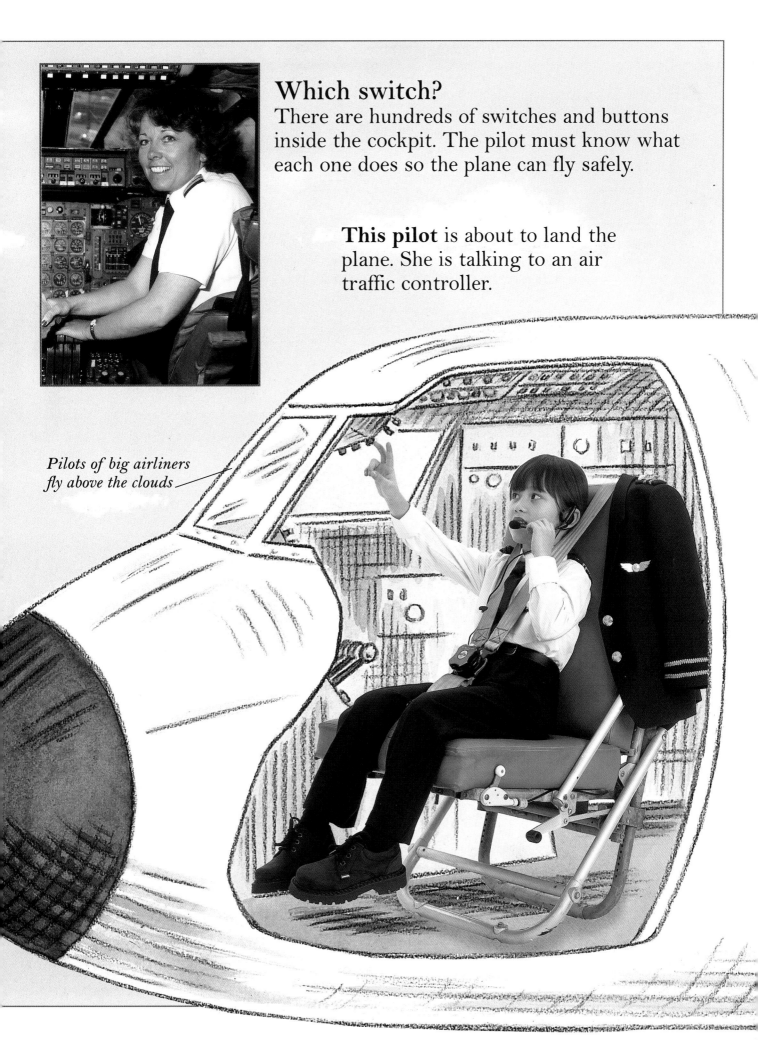

Which switch?

There are hundreds of switches and buttons inside the cockpit. The pilot must know what each one does so the plane can fly safely.

This pilot is about to land the plane. She is talking to an air traffic controller.

Pilots of big airliners fly above the clouds

Paleontologist

Dinosaurs walked the earth 150 million years ago. It's exciting to find out about creatures that lived so long ago by looking at the clues they left behind. I am a paleontologist – a scientist who studies rocks to find fossils of dinosaurs.

I have lots of useful pockets in my vest for tools

Digging for clues
When an important fossil is found it is measured and a note is made of exactly where it was discovered. Then it is dug up and very carefully taken to a laboratory to be studied.

I use a small trowel to help dig up fossils

Back at the lab
A paleontologist spends a lot of time in the laboratory cleaning up and studying fossils. They are often buried deep in rock, and it can take months or even years to clean them up.

How fossils are formed

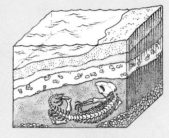

2. Over time, the skeleton sinks beneath the ground.

4. The rock gradually shifts. The fossil may get pushed up to the surface again.

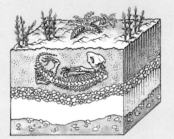

1. When an animal dies, its body decays until only the bones and teeth are left.

3. Over millions of years, the bones turn to rock.

Dinosaurs on display

Fossils can be cleaned up and pieced together to make whole skeletons.

This paleontologist has found some fossils. She is using a sieve to separate them from the sand.

A soft brush is used to carefully remove sand and dust from the fossil

A fossil can not only show you what a creature looked like, but how it lived and what it ate

Rock Star

It's cool being in a rock band. We have lots of fans and go on tour so they can see us play. It's hard work because we travel the world, often staying only one night in each place. It's scary playing in front of thousands of people, but very exciting!

I like to wear trendy denim clothes

I love playing my guitar

I own many different clothes and shoes

Microphone

Compact disc

Singing live!

When a band performs there is a lot of hard work to be done on stage and behind the scenes.

A big screen shows the audience what is happening on stage

Colored lights flash on and off

Huge speakers mean that everyone will hear the music

Spotlights pick out members of the band

In the studio
Bands record songs in a
special studio so their music
can be made into compact
discs and cassettes.

Singing live is
fantastic! This rock
star is performing
in front of some of
her fans.

Microphone

It's showtime!
Popular bands perform
in front of thousands
of people. They often
have amazing light
shows and dramatic
stage sets.

Guitar

Lights

Doctor

I look after patients in a busy hospital. I trained and studied very hard to become a doctor, but it was worth it. My job is tiring, but also rewarding. It feels good to be able to help people get well again.

I always carry my stethoscope with me

I keep notes about all the patients I see

Getting better

Doctors go around to each bed and talk to patients, explaining what is going to happen to them in the hospital. Doctors and nurses work together as part of a team to care for patients.

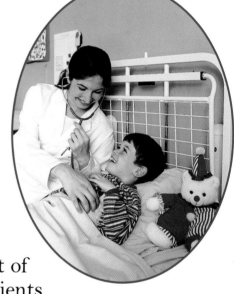

I wear flat, comfortable shoes because I spend a lot of time on my feet

Bandage

Stethoscope

The way things work

Doctors know how all the parts of the body work. When things go wrong, they know what to do to make them better.

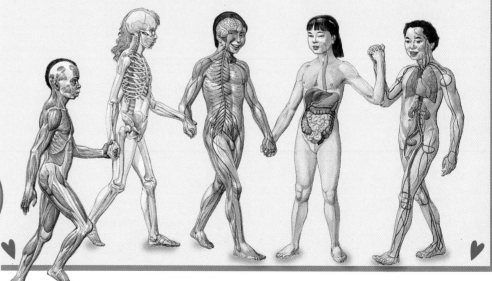

Time to operate

Surgeons are doctors who perform operations. They work in special rooms, repairing broken bones and bodies damaged in accidents.

Emergency!

People who have had serious accidents can be rushed to the hospital in an air ambulance. Special equipment on board means paramedics can treat a patient on the way.

It is important that surgeons have clean hands. They wear gloves while operating

In operating rooms, even your shoes have to be covered! This surgeon is washing her hands, getting ready to operate.

Army Officer

I am an officer in the army. This means that I am trained to lead other soldiers. We are sometimes sent to practice our military skills in very different parts of the world, from a dry, rocky desert to a hot, leafy jungle, because an army needs to be ready to go wherever it is needed. This also gives us the chance to try out specially designed uniforms and equipment.

Water canteen

My boots have steel toes to protect my feet

My binoculars help me to see things that are far away

Helping out

The United Nations peacekeeping force is made up of soldiers from all over the world. If there is a war in any country, they can be sent to help people who may be in trouble.

Blending in

Soldiers wear uniforms printed with different camouflage patterns. This makes it harder for the enemy to see them.

This one is made for a soldier patrolling city streets.

This blends in with the sandy colors of a desert.

This is made for hiding in a forest or jungle.

All together

When men and women join the army they do basic training. Even if they are going to be working as a doctor or a cook, they need to learn how the army works and how to live and work together as a team.

Radio

Identification tag or "dog tag"

Organizing an exercise can be very complicated. This officer is in charge of 30 soldiers. She must make sure each of them have the maps, food, and equipment they need.

Ice Skater

I am getting ready to take part in a big competition. I will be skating on ice to music, wearing a beautiful costume that has been specially made for me. My dream is to one day skate for my country at the Olympic Games.

My clothes are easy to move and dance in

The sparkles on my outfit catch the light as I dance

Practice makes perfect

It takes hours of practice with a coach to get all the moves right. Routines can include jumping, spinning, and even doing the splits!

Perfect pairs

Ice skating is amazing to watch. When two people skate together, their timing must be perfect so they can carry out dramatic lifts and jumps.

First steps

When learning to skate, the easiest way to slow down or stop is to "snowplow."

1

2

1. Glide along with arms out and knees bent, looking straight ahead.

2. Turn heels out and toes inward until you stop.

This skater has just won a competition. She is collecting flowers thrown by her fans.

Rope

Firefighter

My helmet protects my head and neck from fire and falling debris

Firefighting is an exciting job. When the alarm goes off we rush to the fire and try to put it out. Sometimes we have to rescue people from burning buildings. As soon as we arrive we unwind powerful hoses from the fire engine. The hoses blast out foam or water and we begin to fight the fire.

Flashlight

Fire engine

The fire engine is very important because it carries all the equipment needed to fight different fires.

Fireproof fashion

Boots are left in the pant legs so clothes are easy to put on in an emergency.

The clothes that firefighters wear protect them from flames and smoke.

Fluorescent jackets mean they can be seen in the dark.

Breathing equipment is very important when going into burning buildings.

Blazing inferno
Very powerful jets of water are pumped out of hoses so that firefighters can stand far back from the flames.

To the rescue
Firefighters use special cutting equipment if they need to reach someone who is trapped inside a burning building.

Protecting eyes
from smoke and heat is important. This firefighter is wearing a helmet with a visor.

Uniforms are made from material that will not melt or burn

Fashion Designer

I love wearing beautiful clothes, and designing them is great fun. Fashion shows are glamorous and exciting, but lots of people work very hard backstage to make sure the clothes and models look their best.

D F

This is a dress I have designed for next season

On the catwalk

Designers show off their new ideas at fashion shows. We will see similar designs and colors in the stores next season.

Picture this

A fashion designer draws figures wearing her clothes to show the shape and detail of the design. Think about your ideal outfit, then sketch a simple figure like this to show the materials and colors you would use to make it.

I often wear clothes I have designed myself

New looks

A fashion designer has to keep coming up with fresh ideas. She needs to look ahead and plan colors, styles, and fabrics for the seasons ahead.

Paper patterns

When something has been designed, a paper pattern is made and the material is cut. The design is usually made up using plain material first to check that everything looks right.

Dummy

45

This designer is putting the finishing touches to a beautiful dress.

Paper pattern

Scissors

Tape measure

Cutting table

Vet

Scissors

Otoscope

I love all kinds of animals and always wanted to become a veterinarian. I studied hard at college. There is a lot to learn because there are so many different animals that could be brought in for treatment.

I wear a white coat to protect my clothes

Helping hands

Often people bring their pets into the office for a checkup or to have an injection (or shot) to protect them against diseases. Sometimes, though, it is because they are sick or have had an accident.

Sharp teeth!

Some vets are specially trained to look after wild animals, which can be very dangerous. Often these animals are given an injection to make them sleep before they are treated so they won't wake up and attack the vet!

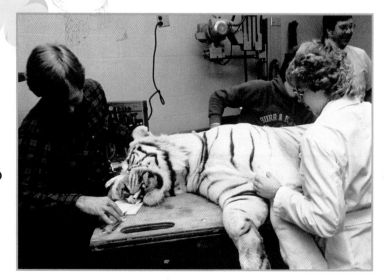

On the farm

Vets treat all kinds of farm animals. They might have to examine a litter of piglets or a whole herd of sheep. If one animal in a herd is sick they must try to protect the others. The vet may have to inject a whole herd of sheep or cows in one day!

Caring for your pet

You can check your pet's eyes, ears, and teeth yourself. It's good for them to get used to being examined at home.

Groom (or brush) your dog or cat several times a week and make sure that an adult treats them for fleas and worms.

A vet wears a white coat when seeing patients in the office and a green gown when operating

This vet is examining an X-ray to check for broken bones.

47

A vet uses a stethoscope, just like a doctor's, to listen to a patient's heartbeat

Your pet may have to wear a plastic collar to prevent it from licking a wound

When visiting the vet's office people often carry their pets in a box or basket

When I grow up
I would like to
be a...

~~Froot~~ Fashion ...

~~hunti~~ Designer.

~~Lily~~